Being Your Best at
Soccer

NEL YOMTOV

Children's Press®
An Imprint of Scholastic Inc.

Content Consultant
Barry Wilner
Associated Press
New York City, New York

Library of Congress Cataloging-in-Publication Data
Names: Yomtov, Nelson.
Title: Being your best at soccer / by Nel Yomtov.
Description: New York : Children's Press An Imprint of Scholastic Inc., 2016. | Series: A True Book |
   Includes bibliographical references and index.
Identifiers: LCCN 2015048544| ISBN 9780531232613 (library binding) | ISBN 9780531236123 (paperback)
Subjects: LCSH: Soccer—Juvenile literature.
Classification: LCC GV943.25 Y65 2015 | DDC 796.334—dc23
LC record available at http://lccn.loc.gov/2015048544

© 2017 Scholastic Inc.
All rights reserved. Published in 2017 by Children's Press, an imprint of Scholastic Inc.
Printed in China 62
SCHOLASTIC, CHILDREN'S PRESS, A TRUE BOOK™, and associated logos are trademarks and/
or registered trademarks of Scholastic Inc.
5 6 7 8 9 10 R 26 25 24 23 22 21 20 19

Scholastic Inc., 557 Broadway, New York, NY 10012.

Front cover: A player performing a scissor kick
Back cover: People playing a soccer game

Find the Truth!

Everything you are about to read is true *except* for one of the sentences on this page.

Which one is **TRUE**?

T or F A player who receives two yellow cards must immediately leave the game.

T or F Soccer originated in the United States.

Find the answers in this book.

Contents

THE **BIG** TRUTH!

Legendary Enemies

A goalkeeper

4

Players during
an indoor
soccer game

Cristiano Ronaldo

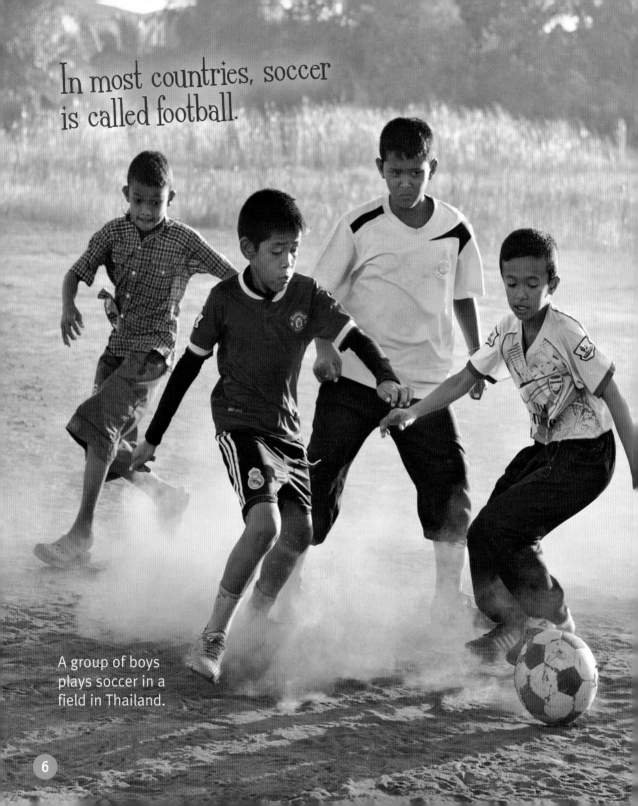

In most countries, soccer is called football.

A group of boys plays soccer in a field in Thailand.

CHAPTER 1

The World's Favorite Sport

Tens of millions of people of all ages in every corner of the world play soccer. From dusty streets and schoolyards to massive stadiums, soccer is the number one sport around the globe. Dating back to ancient China and Greece, soccer has a long and rich history. It is one of the simplest games to learn. Yet it also requires **strategy**, preparation, and teamwork. With practice and a desire for fun, you can become the best soccer player you can be!

Equipment

You don't need lots of fancy, expensive equipment to kick off your soccer career. Of course, you'll need a soccer ball. Wearing a lightweight, loose-fitting shirt and shorts allows you to run, pass, and kick freely. Wear shin guards to protect your lower legs. Put on long, tight-fitting socks over the shin guards. **Cleats** are also an essential part of your gear. They provide **traction** on the field to help you make short stops and sharp turns.

Soccer uniforms are called kits or strips.

Loose-fitting clothes

Tight-fitting socks

Soccer ball

Shin guards

Cleats

A bicycle kick is one of the most difficult soccer moves to pull off.

You Have What It Takes!

Players don't need special skills to begin playing soccer. Children often start playing the sport at four or five years old. Soccer is a fun and exciting game to play, and it provides great exercise for growing bodies. However, speed, **agility**, and **endurance** are the stuff of true soccer stars. Controlling the ball with the feet and the body is essential, but that skill only comes with hard work.

A soccer player takes a corner kick.

It's Called a Pitch

A soccer field is called a pitch. Pitches can be made of natural grass or artificial (human-made) turf. A professional pitch must be at least 98 yards (90 meters) long and no more than 131 yards (120 m) long. The minimum width is 49 yards (45 m), with a maximum of 98 yards (90 m). The fields of youth leagues are often half the size of a professional pitch.

In England, *pitch* is also the name of the field used to play cricket and rugby.

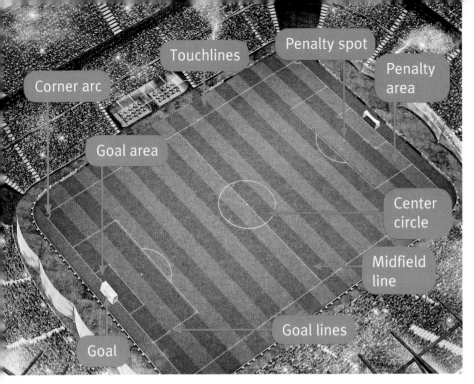

Corner arc

Touchlines

Penalty spot

Penalty area

Goal area

Center circle

Midfield line

Goal lines

Goal

Knowing the different parts of the pitch is an important part of understanding soccer.

Reading a Soccer Field

If you're "in the game," the chalk markings on a soccer pitch are important to know.

- ⚽ *Midfield line*: divides the playing field in half
- ⚽ *Touchlines*: run the length of the field, marking the sides of the field
- ⚽ *Goal lines*: mark each end of the playing field at their width
- ⚽ *Center circle*: marks the kickoff for starting the game and for restarting it after goals and halftime

- *Goal*: the structure into which players aim the ball to score

- ***Penalty*** *area*: a box 18 yards (16.5 m) deep and 44 yards (40 m) long; penalty kicks are taken from within this area at the penalty spot

- *Goal area*: a box within the penalty area measuring 6 yards (5.5 m) by 20 yards (18 m), from which **defending** teams take goal kicks

- *Corner arc*: the area from which attacking teams take corner kicks; one is located in each corner of the field

A lot of action occurs in the goal areas.

Each player on a
soccer team plays
an important role
in the game.

CHAPTER **3**

Who's Who

Each soccer team has 11 players: 1 goalkeeper and 10 position players. The offensive team, called the attacking team, controls the ball. The defensive team is the team without the ball. The object of the game is to kick the ball past the goalkeeper and into the goal. Each position on the pitch requires special skills.

 An indoor soccer game is played on an artificial turf field with six players on each team.

The Goalie: Guts and Glory

The goalkeeper is sometimes called the goalie or keeper. Goalies are the only ones allowed to touch the ball with their hands inside the field of play. They wear gloves to protect their hands and help them catch or **deflect** shots. If a goalie catches the ball, he or she must throw it or kick it within six seconds. Goalies must be agile and not afraid to make jumping, diving, and sliding saves.

A goalie jumps to deflect a shot at the goal.

Goalkeepers' Gloves

Amadeo Carrizo is believed to have been the first goalkeeper to wear gloves. Carrizo played in Argentina in the 1940s and 1950s. As the years passed, goalie gloves became more common. At first, many goalkeepers wore them only in wet conditions to better grip the wet ball. By the 1980s, gloves were an essential piece of soccer equipment. Modern manufacturers make gloves using a variety of fabrics and rubber. Today, even some field players wear gloves on the pitch.

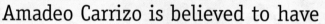

A goalie reaches for the ball.

Guarding one opposing player is called man-to-man defense.

Sometimes players might slide on the ground to perform a tackle.

Defenders

The defenders, or fullbacks, help the goalie protect the team's goal. They are positioned in front of the goalie to keep the other team from setting up and taking good shots. Defenders must be skilled at tackling, or intercepting, the ball. Sometimes defenders guard particular players on the other team. Other times, they defend a particular area of the field.

Forwards

Forwards, or attackers, are speedy players who can handle the ball well and try to score. They usually take passes from midfielders or defenders on their team and then rush to attack the opponent's goal. Forwards must have outstanding **dribbling** skills to avoid oncoming defenders from the other team. The center forward is called a striker. This person is usually the team's top goal scorer.

A forward prepares to take a shot on goal.

Midfielders

Midfielders, or halfbacks, cover the middle of the field. They play both defense and offense. On defense, they help defenders guard the goal. On offense, they pass the ball to forwards who are racing downfield to the opponent's goal. Midfielders must be good tacklers and passers. Because they run more than any other player on the pitch, midfielders must have tremendous endurance.

Midfielders must be extremely good all-around players.

Basic Soccer Formations

A formation is the way a soccer team positions its players on the pitch. One of the most common formations is a strong defensive setup called the 4-4-2. Four defenders

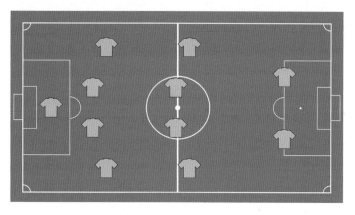

A 4-4-2 formation

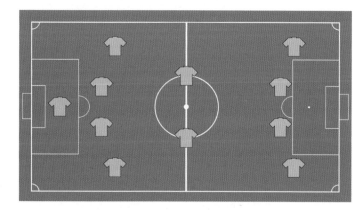

A 4-2-4 formation

are in front of the goalie, and four midfielders cover the midfield line. Two forwards remain downfield to attack. The 4-2-4 formation is designed to create a powerful offensive attack. Four defenders cover the goalie. Two midfielders and four forwards pressure the opposing team's defense.

Legendary Enemies

Rivalries between soccer teams are famous. Their games, called derbies, are major events. Some rivalries extend beyond the pitch, inspiring fights, violence, and even riots among fans. These rivalries are often not just about the game. They may also come out of political, regional, and other differences.

El Clásico

The rivalry between Real (ray-AL) Madrid and Barcelona in Spain is one of the world's most intense. It even has a nickname: *El Clásico*, or "The Classic." The bitter competition is based on a history of political differences. Barcelona is in Catalonia, a region that has long fought to separate from Spain and its capital, Madrid. As of 2015, Real Madrid has won 92 matches to Barcelona's 90.

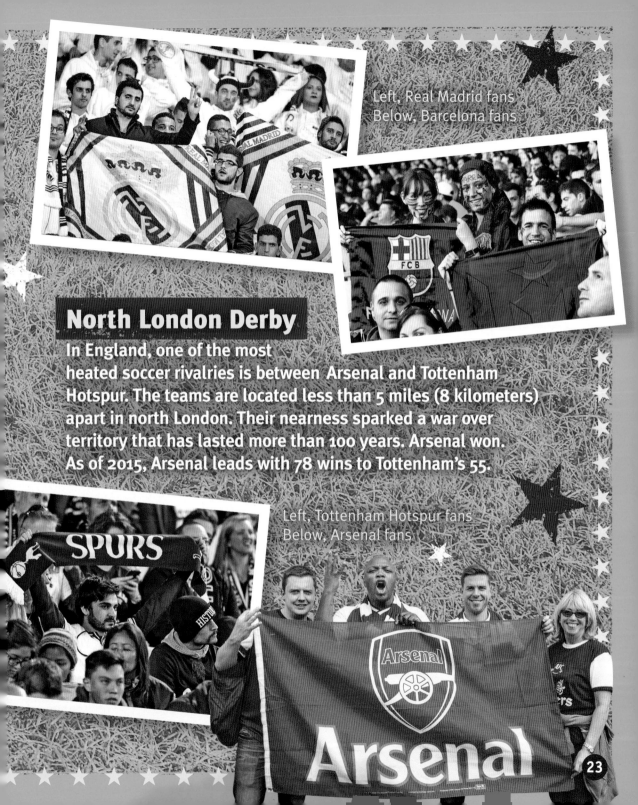

Left, Real Madrid fans
Below, Barcelona fans

North London Derby

In England, one of the most
heated soccer rivalries is between Arsenal and Tottenham
Hotspur. The teams are located less than 5 miles (8 kilometers)
apart in north London. Their nearness sparked a war over
territory that has lasted more than 100 years. Arsenal won.
As of 2015, Arsenal leads with 78 wins to Tottenham's 55.

Left, Tottenham Hotspur fans
Below, Arsenal fans

The International Federation of Association Football (FIFA) governs soccer internationally.

Following the Rules

A soccer game lasts 90 minutes, divided into two 45-minute halves. At the start of the second half, the teams switch sides of the field. If the score is tied, most games simply end in a draw. During the World Cup (soccer's top competition), officials may add two 15-minute periods. If the score is still tied after that, both teams do penalty kicks. One referee and two assistants oversee the game. A fourth official displays the playing time and makes sure teams follow the rules when substituting a player.

Let the Game Begin!

A game starts with a kickoff from the field's center. During the game, play pauses if the ball leaves the field. If it crosses a sideline, the attacking team performs a throw-in, tossing the ball overhead into the field. The ball sometimes crosses the goal line without entering the goal. If an attacker last touched the ball, the goalie kicks the ball back into play. If a defender last touched it, the attacking team makes a corner kick.

A goalie prepares to kick the ball back into play after it went out of bounds.

Tripping an opponent can lead to injuries on the field.

Fouls and Misconduct

No players except goalies are allowed to touch the ball with their hands in the field of play. Kicking, pushing, tripping, charging, and striking an opponent are also against the rules. Certain serious offenses are called misconduct. These include arguing with the officials and delaying the restarting of play. So is pretending to be hurt to get an opponent in trouble. Entering, reentering, and leaving the field without the referee's permission are also illegal.

Penalties

A referee punishes players guilty of misconduct or committing a foul. The referee shows the player a yellow card as a warning. If the player continues illegal behavior, he or she is shown another yellow card, then a red card. The player must then leave the field. That person's team continues with one less player. A referee may send someone directly off the field with no warnings in cases of violent or abusive behavior.

A red card is the strongest penalty a referee can issue.

During a penalty kick, the goalie must stay on the goal line until the kick has been made.

Free Kicks and Penalty Kicks

Free kicks are awarded to victims of fouls and misconduct. In a direct free kick, a team shoots directly at the goal. With an indirect free kick, one player must touch the ball before another can shoot a goal. A penalty kick occurs if a player commits a foul inside the penalty area in front of his or her team's goal. With only the goalie defending, a player on the opposing team kicks at the goal.

Performing drills is a great way to improve ball-handling skills.

Get in the Game!

The only way to become the best soccer player you can be is to practice. There are no shortcuts to becoming a great player. It takes dedication and hard work. Work on skills you already have *and* develop new ones. Always warm up before you play or practice. Running side to side and running sprints will strengthen your legs and build endurance. Don't forget to stretch your legs—they do most of the work on the pitch!

FIFA has 209 member countries.

Dribbling

One of the most important soccer skills is dribbling. Great dribblers use the entire foot—sides, top, and bottom—to gently tap the ball in front of them. Practice dribbling first using only one foot. Tap the ball with the inside of your foot. Follow the ball and tap it again, and then continue following and tapping. As you gain confidence, try using the other foot to tap the ball.

Being able to dribble effectively with both feet is one of the most important skills in the game.

Passing

Accurate passing is essential to moving the ball downfield or getting the ball to your teammate. To make a basic pass, see your target and approach the ball. Plant your nonkicking foot on the ground. Your toes should point in the direction you want to kick the ball. Focus on the ball and quickly kick it with the inside of your other foot. Follow through toward the target.

A player might pass the ball quickly to the side using the outside of his or her foot.

Player hits with her heel to kick the ball back

Pass the ball to a teammate behind you with a heel pass.

Other types of passes require different skills.

⚽ *Heel pass:* To pass to a teammate behind you, make contact with the center of the ball with your heel. Generate power from your knee down. Do not follow through.

⚽ *Outside foot pass:* This technique can be used for passing and shooting. Kick the lower, outside part of the ball if you want the ball to go high. Kick the top part if you want it to travel low.

International Soccer Competitions

Men's soccer first appeared in the Olympic Games in 1900. Women's soccer was added in 1996. Since then, the women's U.S. team has dominated, winning gold in almost every Olympics.

The World Cup is an international, monthlong soccer competition held every four years. The men's **tournament** began in 1930, the women's in 1991. Thirty-two national teams play in the men's World Cup. In the women's, 24 national teams compete.

Chest Trapping

Chest trapping is the most effective way to bring the ball out of the air. First, rise up on your toes. Hold your arms out for balance. Lean back slightly as the ball hits your chest, to cushion and absorb the impact. Lean forward to pop the ball up and drop it to the ground. Don't let the ball bounce away from you. Keep the ball at your feet, where you can control it.

Timeline of Soccer History

5000–300 BCE
Athletes play a soccerlike game in ancient China.

1863 CE
The Football Association forms in England to establish a set of rules for London teams.

1872
Scotland plays England in the first official international soccer match.

On the Defense

Great defensive skills are the key to slowing an opponent's attack. Move quickly to the ball carrier. This puts pressure on that player. When the player is close, slow down. If you rush the ball carrier, he or she could make a quick cut around you. Keep your knees bent and your arms up for balance. Make a tackle only when you're sure you can take the ball. If you fail to make the tackle, reenter play quickly.

1900

Male athletes play soccer in the Olympic Games for the first time.

1930

FIFA holds the first World Cup tournament.

1996

The U.S. women's team wins the first-ever women's soccer tournament at the Olympics.

Pelé made the bicycle kick (shown here) famous.

CHAPTER 6

A Gallery of Greats

Many people consider Pelé, or Edson Arantes do Nascimento, the greatest soccer player of all time. Playing for his home country, Brazil, Pelé won three World Cups. He scored 757 career goals in 812 official games. Counting games outside of standard league play, he made 1,283 goals in 1,393 games. Fast and agile, Pelé is best remembered as a superb striker and dribbler. But he is just one of many soccer greats.

Pelé played his first professional game at the age of 15.

Women Superstars

Mia Hamm is among the most famous Americans ever in soccer. Playing forward, she helped the U.S. team win the Women's World Cup in 1991 and 1999. She was also a member of the team that won Olympic gold in 1996 and 2004. Hamm's teammate

Abby Wambach is the U.S. team's all-time leading goal scorer, with 184 goals since 2001. Wambach was a member of the 2004 Olympic and 2015 World Cup winning teams.

Mia Hamm is widely considered to be one of the greatest soccer players of all time.

Sun Wen prepares to take a shot in a 2000 game against Australia.

Sun Wen played with the women's Chinese national soccer team during the 1990s. In 2000, she was co-winner of the FIFA Female Player of the Century award with American Michelle Akers. Nadine Angerer was a member of the German team that won the Women's World Cup in 2003 and 2007. In 2014, she was named FIFA World Player of the Year. She was the first goalkeeper— male or female—to win the honor.

Lionel Messi heads the ball into the air in a 2015 game against Germany's Bayer 04 Leverkusen team.

Masterly Men

Lionel Messi is one of today's greatest soccer stars. Born in Argentina, Messi is a five-time winner of the FIFA Player of the Year, or Ballon d'Or, award. In 2008, he led Argentina to a gold medal at the Olympic Games. Playing with the Barcelona club of Spain, he has won 14 championships. He's also helped the team capture FIFA Club World championships in 2009 and 2011.

Portuguese-born Cristiano Ronaldo plays for Real Madrid in Spain and Portugal's national team. An exceptional dribbler and goal scorer, he is one of the world's finest forwards.

Johan Cruyff is considered by many experts to be Europe's most talented player of all time. In a career that spanned from 1964 to 1984, the Dutch forward won numerous European championships. After retiring from active play, he became a successful coach. All of these players are great examples of being your best at soccer. ★

Cristiano Ronaldo is famous for his acrobatic moves on the field.

True Statistics

Largest attendance at a single soccer match: 199,854, Maracaña Stadium, Brazil (1950)

Average distance a professional soccer player runs in a soccer match: 7 mi. (11 km)

Most goals scored in a match by one player: 16 (twice, by Stephan Stanis and Panagiotis Pontikos)

Number of active players and referees associated with FIFA worldwide: 265 million players and 5 million referees

Number of people worldwide on average who watch the World Cup on television: 3.2 billion

Size of the FIFA World Cup trophy: 14.5 in. (36.8 cm) high and 13.4 lb. (6.1 kg)

Did you find the truth?

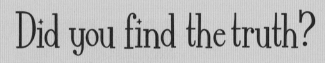

T A player who receives two yellow cards must immediately leave the game.

F Soccer originated in the United States.

Resources

Books

Crisfield, Deborah. *The Everything Kids' Soccer Book: Rules, Techniques, and More About Your Favorite Sport!* Avon, MA: Adams Media, 2015.

Jökulsson, Illugi. *Stars of Women's Soccer.* New York: Abbeville Press, 2015.

Visit this Scholastic Web site for more information on being your best at soccer:

★ www.factsfornow.scholastic.com
Enter the keywords **Being Your Best at Soccer**

Important Words

agility (uh-JIL-ih-tee) the ability to move fast and easily

cleats (KLEETS) shoes that have metal or wooden spikes fastened to the bottom of them to prevent slipping

defending (di-FEND-ing) trying to keep an opposing side or team from scoring points

deflect (di-FLEKT) to make something go in a different direction

dribbling (DRIB-ling) controlling a soccer ball with the feet while walking or running

endurance (en-DOOR-uhns) the ability to do something difficult for a long time

penalty (PEN-uhl-tee) a punishment a team or player suffers for breaking a rule

rivalries (RYE-vuhl-reez) fierce competitions between two or more people or groups

strategy (STRAT-i-jee) a clever plan for winning a game or achieving a goal

tournament (TOOR-nuh-muhnt) a series of contests in which a number of people or teams try to win the championship

traction (TRAK-shuhn) the force that keeps a moving body from slipping on a surface

Index

Page numbers in **bold** indicate illustrations.

About the Author

Nel Yomtov is an award-winning author with a passion for writing nonfiction books for young readers. He has written books and graphic novels about history, geography, science, and other subjects.

Nel has worked at Marvel Comics, where he edited, wrote, and colored hundreds of titles. He has also served as editorial director of a children's book publisher and as publisher of Hammond World Atlas books.

Yomtov lives in the New York City area with his wife, Nancy, a teacher. Their son, Jess, is a sports journalist.